ARE YOU SAVED ?

The Orthodox Christian Process of Salvation

D0063901

FIFTH EDITION

ARE YOU SAVED ?

The Orthodox Christian Process of Salvation

by
Barbara Pappas

Introduction by
Rev. William S. Chiganos

Amnos Publications

By the same author:
First and Second Corinthians: a Study of Paul's Letters
ISBN 978-1-928653-25-7
Regina Orthodox Press, Salisbury, MA

God's Bubbly, Gurgly, Overwhelming, Overflowing Love
(A Children's Book for All Ages)
ISBN 978-0-9623721-6-2
Amnos Publications, Westchester, Il.

Cover icon, illustrating Christ's Descent into Hades, was written by Rev. Irinej (Dobrivejec)—see page 54.

Library of Congress Catalog Card Number 95-79640
ISBN 978-0-9623721-7-9

First Edition: July 1984
Second Printing: October 1984
Second Edition: January 1987
Third (Expanded) Edition: June 1995
Fourth Edition (Expanded): July 1997
Fifth Edition: November 2006
1 2 3 4 5 6 7 8 9 – 12 11 10 09 08 07 06

Amnos Publications
Holy Apostles Greek Orthodox Church
2501 South Wolf Road
Westchester, Illinois 60154
(708) 562-2706
Fax: (708) 562-2752
email: ayspappas@comcast.net

To
Dad and Peter
in loving memory

ACKNOWLEDGMENTS

A work about salvation would not be complete without an acknowledgement of the synergistic role of the Theotokos, Mother of God. She accepted God's will for her life without concern for the heartache it would bring to her days on earth. We marvel at her strength and love.

Metropolitan Iakovos of Chicago, Metropolitan Isaiah of Denver, Rev. William S. Chiganos, Rev. Dr. Stanley S. Harakas and Rev. George Nicozisin read the original manuscript of this work and offered valuable suggestions. Carolyn Skoirchet and Nola Vandarakis edited it critically yet lovingly. Ann Lampros offered her much needed special expertise in publishing. Linda Hardy continues to be of invaluable assistance with the tedious technical aspects of updating each new printing or edition.

Icons illustrating the four steps in the salvation process are the work of Ger. S. Manettas and Sons, Athens, Greece, and are used by permission of "God is With Us" Publications, McKees Rocks, Pa.

CONTENTS

INTRODUCTION

Thankfully, an ever-increasing number of our Orthodox faithful, young and old alike, continue to discuss openly a subject that for a long time had been avoided. Questions such as, *Are you saved?*, *What is meant by salvation?*, *What must I do to be saved?* are being asked in Sunday School, in Bible study groups and in prayer circles. I view this growing interest and unrest as a sign of spiritual growth. "All of creation groans" to know the truth.

Most have associated such talk with Protestantism and the "born-again" Christian. Until relatively recently, most of our faithful avoided such discussions because of lack of knowledge about the subject of salvation. This topic is not new to our faith. A study of ecclesiastical history and the various battles waged by the Fathers of the early Church reveals that the question of "being saved" was just as relevant in the times of John Chrysostom, Gregory of Nyssa and others, as it is today.

This study will help everyone who reads it to have a working knowledge of salvation through Jesus Christ and to be able to discuss it with those around them. It is not an attempt to provide easy answers for this all-important topic. Rather, it is a labor of love by a teacher of the faith who has dealt with it personally and who has been called upon by her peers and her students to provide answers and guidelines. This is not the final manual on the subject but a window through which the restless soul may be led to the harbor of truth and understanding concerning salvation.

The author of this work, Barbara Pappas, was motivated to prepare this work because she is concerned for the salvation not only of her own soul but also those of her brethren. Dostoyevsky's Starets Zossima, in *The Brothers Karamazov,* comes closer to the truth when he says that we are, each of us, "responsible for everyone and everything."

Barbara Pappas has served as a Sunday School teacher and as the Curriculum Director for the Holy Apostles Church School in Westchester, Illinois for many years, during which time she has worked with teachers, parents and youngsters of all ages. She is presently a member of the Religious Education Commission of the Greek Orthodox Metropolis of Chicago and teaches adult Bible Study at Holy Apostles. Drawing upon these experiences, she put together the following careful and prayerful study. All who have come in contact with her have benefited from her radiant love for the Church, her unshakable faith in Jesus Christ as the promised Messiah, her deep understanding of the Orthodox faith and her insatiable desire to share God's revealed truths with others. It is a privilege and a distinct pleasure to call her one of the faithful servants in Christ's Church.

We reiterate our gratitude for the unstinting support of this work offered by the late Archbishop Iakovos of North and South America when it was first introduced, as well as to our Beloved Metropolitan Iakovos of Chicago, Metropolitan Isaiah of Denver and other leading churchmen who have also endorsed it from the beginning and continue to stand behind it.

I recommend this book to everyone who thirsts for knowledge and truth. I believe it is a welcome and useful tool for personal study, for Sunday School discussions and for prayer and Bible study groups. Read it in its entirety and then return to the sections that interest you most. It has much to offer for your enrichment and understanding of our timeless and precious Orthodox faith.

Reverend William S. Chiganos
Chairman, Religious Education Commission
Metropolis of Chicago

Chapter One

ICON OF THE NATIVITY

This icon points to the first step in the salvation process: We must "Believe," that Jesus Christ is the Messiah, whose birth on earth as man fulfilled all prophesies and promises of the Old Testament. He defeated the Devil and provided *The Way* into God's Eternal Kingdom.

What shall we bring to You, O Christ, Who for our sakes was born on earth as man? Every creature made by You offers You thanks. The angels offer a hymn; the heavens a star; the wise men, gifts; the shepherds, amazement; the earth its cave; and we— the Virgin Mother. O pre-eternal God, have mercy upon us.

From Eve of Nativity Vespers

By three stars, one on the front of her head-covering and one on each shoulder, Orthodox iconography reflects the fact that Mary remained a virgin before, during and after she conceived Christ, in fulfillment of prophecy. He took on flesh to save us from the wiles of the Devil, depicted in the lower-left corner of the icon of the Nativity in the guise of a shepherd trying to put doubts in Joseph's mind as to who the Child's father might be. The blackness of the cave in which Christ was born symbolizes the evil of the world into which He came and to which He brought the light of truth.

Come, let us greatly rejoice in the Lord as we sing of this present mystery. The wall which divided God from man has been destroyed. The flaming sword withdraws from Eden's gate; the cherubim withdraw from the Tree of Life, and I, who had been cast out through my disobedience, now feast on the delights of paradise: For today the Father's perfect Image, marked with the stamp of His eternity, has taken the form of a servant. Without undergoing change He is born from an unwedded mother; He was true God, and He remains the same, but through His love for mankind, He has become what He never was: true man! Come, O faithful, let us cry to Him: O God, born of a virgin, have mercy on us!

From Eve of Nativity Vespers
The Services of Christmas
Orthodox Church in America

Chapter One

GOD'S DIVINE PLAN

If the desire of the Heavenly Kingdom burns in your soul like a lighted torch, be sure your soul will quickly become its heir, Abba Iperechus tells us.

Archimandrite Chrysostomos
The Ancient Fathers of the Desert

ARE YOU SAVED?

What is the Orthodox response to this most important question? The Bible provides the basis for the answer we seek, but scripture can be misinterpreted. The historic Church addressed this problem by preserving, for all generations, the eternal truths received from Christ and the Apostles. The vehicles used for this sacred task are the writings of early Church Fathers, decisions of Councils (which refuted heresies), Liturgics, Hymnology and Iconography. As in any quest for theological truth, our guide is the consensus found in these treasures.

The Old Testament records that *in the beginning, God created the heavens and the earth* and everything visible and invisible. Then He looked around at what He had done and *saw that it was good* (Gen 1: 25). Out of the great love that He embodies, for God is love, He wanted to share what He had created. But He did not want to surround Himself with robots—creatures who could respond to Him only as programmed. Because only beings like Himself would fully appreciate the wonders of that which He had to give, He created man and woman *in His image*, which includes free will. He gave them dominion over the earth and every living thing.[1] All He asked in return was their love—a phenomenon made possible by free will—the only thing that was truly theirs to give.

The Lord God planted a garden eastward in Eden, and there He put the man [and the woman] *He had formed* (Gen 2:8). It was perfect. God walked with them. He talked with them.[2] They were surrounded by wonder, beauty, and every good thing to eat and had the potential to grow into full

15

fellowship with their Creator.[3] Along the way they had the blessing of meaningful work to do—tending of the garden—unhampered by the toil and tedium that can make life and work frustrating. There was no disease for man, animal or plant; no old age and death to contemplate; nothing to mar the serenity of the garden or their lives. To complete the perfect growing conditions for all living things, God provided a continual mist which came up from the earth to nourish the Garden, and all was in perfect harmony.

Surely Adam and Eve must have professed great love for their gracious benefactor, but words are not enough. True love requires choice. So God gave Adam and Eve freedom to do as they pleased—with one exception. As a way to demonstrate their love and to strengthen them through self discipline, He told them not to eat of the *tree of the knowledge of good and evil* (Gen 2:17). Then He *allowed* Satan to tempt them.

The results were disastrous. Adam and Eve failed to keep the one commandment they had been given, succumbing instead to the same form of greed and pride that had caused Satan's fall from Heaven.[4] In the hearts that should have been filled with love and gratitude for all God had made possible for them, there grew instead an overwhelming desire to be as He was, without limitation. Rejecting the constant struggle that obedience and growth in God's image would entail, they opted rather to try to take His place through disobedience—to unseat Him from His throne—which is impossible.

> The Tree of Knowledge was not forbidden because God grudged it to man...It would have been good if partaken of at the proper time; for the Tree was, according to my theory, contemplation, which is safe only for those who have reached maturity, not for those who are still somewhat simple and greedy; just as neither is solid food good for those who are yet tender and have need of milk.
> GREGORY OF NAZIANZUS[5]

The consequence of disobedience was death. Adam and Eve had been created to live forever, but now God clothed them in *tunics of skin* (Gen 3:21), the mortality that would put limits on everything they had known.[6] Then He drove them out of the

16

garden and placed Cherubim and a flaming sword at the gate so they could not get back in to eat from the Tree of Life.

From then on, the first man and woman had to fend for themselves. No longer in the protected environment of the garden, they would have to toil for their food and battle the thorns and thistles of life: potential problems with the weather, the animals (who, until then, had been their friends), one another and everything else the Devil could put in their paths.[7] They would struggle with aging, illness and unleashed evil. In this setting, death, which loomed on the horizon, would actually be a blessing. It would cast a shadow on the joys of life but would also set boundaries to the effects of the fallen world. Personal suffering and the opportunity to cause others to suffer would be contained by the fragility of life and the limits of time. Since we are descendants of Adam and Eve, we are inheritors of the conditions brought about by their "original sin" and eviction from paradise.[8] The joy of life is that it offers the opportunity to return to the blessed state Adam and Eve lost for all of us.

Salvation is the return to assurance of eternal life with God in the idyllic state that surrounds Him. Our earthly life is a precious gift in that it is our one and only chance to avail ourselves of this deliverance. God's promise to us, however, is not the original garden but Heaven itself where, in His very presence,[9] there will be no more temptation and no more capacity for or possibility of sin. The time of testing and separating of those who love God from those who do not will have come to an end. To waste this opportunity for salvation is to consign ourselves to the agony of profound regret.[10] But regret that comes after death is too late. It becomes the *worm that does not die* (Mk 9:46), the *unquenchable fire* that eternally burns within (Mt 3:12).

GOD'S PROMISES

Before God evicted Adam and Eve from Eden, He offered them the comfort of the first prophecy,[11] revealing His Fatherly, ever-abiding love for and confidence in man, despite man's sinfulness. God promised to send His Son, Jesus Christ (the *Seed* of the *Woman*, the Theotokos, through the

Holy Spirit), Who would redeem man from the effects of that which, with Satan's prodding, he had done to himself. Christ would do battle with the Devil, the originator of sin and father of lies.[12] Satan would be a constant annoyance to Christ, but in spite of all his efforts, would succeed only in bruising Christ's *heel* (with Crucifixion). In the end, Christ would be victorious with a fatal blow to Satan's *head* (through His Resurrection). This promised divine Redeemer would come *in the fullness of time* (Gal 4:4), after God had given man a chance to recognize his need for a Savior.

To convince man of this great need, God set in motion His Divine Plan, which contained three major elements,[13] each of which brought those who were willing further along the road to salvation. First He established the ORAL COVENANT, through Abraham, under which Abraham's people would be God's people, if they would obey Him.[14] The sign of this covenant was circumcision; its purpose was to demonstrate the necessity for God's people to be different—set apart from the rest of the world—and to establish a nation (Israel) and a family from that nation (the family of David) through which salvation (Jesus Christ) would come. However, instead of obeying God, most of Abraham's people turned away from Him; instead of bringing the pagans to God, they joined the pagans.

> The history of the Old Testament is that of elections linked to successive falls. Through these God saves a "remnant" whose patient waiting purifies...until the supreme purity of the Virgin is capable of giving birth to the Savior of humanity.[15]

In time, when man was ready, God took the next step, establishing the WRITTEN COVENANT, the "Law," through Moses. The purpose of this "Mosaic" Law was to define sin by outlining perfection, that which was required to return to the presence of God. This experience would show man that he could never earn salvation on his own.[16] Adam and Eve had one commandment to keep; now there were ten.[17] In addition, there were 613 laws,[18] each of which had to be kept precisely— to break one was to break them all.[19] Each transgression had

18

to be followed by a related offering or sacrifice to establish the fact that sin (defined under this covenant as the breaking of the Law) required atonement. Man was caught in a never-ending cycle: he would inevitably break a law, bring the required offering, and go out and break another. This futile repetition continued until—finally—Jesus Christ offered Himself as the last living sacrifice on behalf of all mankind.[20]

God told the Israelites to build an ark to house the tablets upon which He had written the Ten Commandments, and a Tabernacle (later replaced by the Temple) to house the ark. The ark was to be kept in the sacred area called the Most Holy Place, where God was present among His people.[21] Only the High Priest could enter this *Holy of Holies*, and then only once a year, on the Day of Atonement, to offer sacrificial blood, which pre-figured the redemptive Blood that Christ would offer, and to beg forgiveness for the sins of the people.[22] The Most Holy Place was separated by a veil from the area called the Holy Place,[23] where Old Testament priests offered the sacrifices of the people to God daily in accordance with the Law. The veil between the Holy Place and the Most Holy Place symbolized the fact that because of disobedience man had created a barrier between himself and God.[24]

God allowed His people to feel the hopelessness of trying to save themselves through the Law, but He never allowed them to fall into despair. Throughout Old Testament times, He continually gave them signs and prophecies about the coming of the Messiah, Who would deliver them from their terrible predicament.

Man's need for a Savior. Scripture records that Enoch and Elijah were taken directly into Heaven because they pleased God.[25] St. John Chrysostom relates that Elijah was perfect, not in the complete sense that Christ was but in relation to his time in history.[26] Though we are all called to be perfect,[27] the rest of us probably fall far short of the mark, which is the definition of sin (Greek: *amartia*).

We therefore *need* a Savior, a Mediator to do for us what we cannot do for ourselves. When man had been given sufficient time to understand this fact, God kept His promise: He sent His Son, Who, in His two natures, truly God and truly man, bridged the gap between Heaven and earth[28] and became

19

the ladder of Jacob's dream, the instrument by which we can climb to Heaven.[29]

Our Lord lived a perfect life, satisfying the condition of obedience God expects from those who want to dwell with Him eternally. He thus fulfilled the Law and legalistically *earned* salvation. Throughout Christ's ministry, His enemies had tried to have Him killed,[30] but He thwarted their efforts until the time was right.[31] Satan salivated at the prospect of the death of the Son of God, but it is clear that Christ was in control. At the time set by God, Christ surrendered His life willingly, for that is what He had come to do.[32] But by engineering Christ's death, Satan overstepped his bounds and fell into a divine trap.

> On the hook of His divinity, the humanity of Christ is the bait; the Devil throws himself on the prey, but the hook pierces Him—he cannot swallow God... GREGORY OF NYSSA[33]

Christ passed through death, but it could not hold Him because He was sinless! Thus He resurrected, through God's overriding power–foiling Satan and overcoming death in the process.

> As long as sin sentenced only the guilty to death, no interference with it was possible, seeing that it had justice on its side. But when it subjected to the same punishment Him Who was innocent, guiltless, and worthy of crowns of honor and hymns of praise...it was stripped of its power.
>
> CYRIL OF ALEXANDRIA[34]

The death of Christ was not a price God set for man's redemption but rather the consequence of sin inherited by all who lived after Adam and Eve. In taking on human form, Christ also knowingly took on man's legacy of suffering and death. The deaths of those who lived before Christ, however, were justified because all had sinned. There was no justification for Christ's death, but as the perfect sacrificial Lamb,[35] He willingly assumed the burden of the sins of man. As His life ebbed on the Cross, the sky darkened and the earth quaked. The downward spiral of creation had been reversed. The veil in the Temple tore in two because Christ's redeeming death removed the barrier of sin between God and man, giving man, once again, access to God.[36]

> To whom was the Blood offered which was shed for us, and for what purpose was it shed, this great and precious Blood of our God Who was both Priest and Victim? For we were held in bondage by the Wicked One, sold under the dominion of sin, receiving instead the pleasure of wickedness. But if the price of redemption is paid to the one who holds the bond, to whom, I ask, was it offered, and Why? If to the Wicked One: then alas for the loss of it! If the thief receives, not alone from God, but also God Himself as ransom, it would have been more equitable to have saved the payment of so great a price in exchange for his tyranny. If it was paid to the Father first, how was this done? For we were not held in bondage by Him. And again, why should the Blood of His only-Begotten Son be acceptable to the Father, Who would not accept Isaac when he was offered by his father but instead changed the sacrifice, substituting a ram in the place of the rational victim? (Gen 22:13).
>
> Is it not plain that the Father accepted It, but that He neither demanded It, nor had need of It; but because of the Plan of Redemption...
> GREGORY OF NAZIANZUS[37]

Christ had brought others, like Lazarus, back to life, but only temporarily—they faced death again. Our Lord became the first-fruits of the dead[38] because He would die no more. After walking the earth for forty days so His Apostles and disciples could see Him, know that He was indeed alive again, and be assured that there is life after death, He ascended to His Throne at the right hand of His Father, where He waits for those who love Him.

The third and final BLOOD COVENANT with God was thus established as the fulfillment of the Oral and Written Covenants before it. In keeping with its provisions, all who *believe* that Jesus Christ is the Son of God and accept and confess that He is their Lord and Savior, the promised Messiah Who provided the way to the eternal Kingdom, will receive the gift of salvation. They are the new Israel, the adopted seed of Abraham through Christ (Gal 3:29), redeemed once and for all from the effects of sin,[39] not by their own efforts but by virtue of being a part of Christ through Baptism, Eucharist, and a life of faith, thus enabled to enjoy God's promises with Him (share His inheritance.)[40]

Belief must be proved. It is very easy to say, "I believe." It is much harder to live accordingly—yet that is the true test. Even "demons believe" (Jas 2:19) but reject the required obedience. Thus Christ said, *Not everyone who says to me "Lord, Lord," shall enter the Kingdom of Heaven, but he who does the will of my Father* (Mt 7:21). Scripture is very clear in making the point that we cannot just profess faith and thereafter feel confident of salvation. Faith must be proved by a life lived according to the word of God because *faith without works is dead* (Jas 2:20). Those who object that God knows whether or not we have faith so there is no need to "prove" it should consider Paul's words in 2 Cor 13:5.

> Every day and every hour, proof is demanded of us of our love of God. For God, every day and every hour, proves His love for us.
> ISAAC THE SYRIAN[41]

Certainly God knows the intentions of our hearts. The requirement that we demonstrate faith during our lives is for our benefit—not His. It is a blessing, not a burden. It helps us guard against complacency. It stirs us to action and prods us toward holiness, that we might rise above human nature and become *partakers of the divine nature* through the acquisition of virtue, knowledge, self-control, perseverance, godliness, kindness and love in addition to our faith. Scripture promises that *if* we participate in this struggle for spiritual growth to the extent we are able, we will be allowed to enter *into the everlasting Kingdom of our Lord and Savior, Jesus Christ* (2 Pet 1:5-11).

A young Abbot was counseled thus, in our own day, by a Holy man: *Today many people, wishing for an excuse not to do what God asks of them, find fault with the teaching of the Holy Church and reject correct Christian belief. Instead, they choose to believe what they wish. This is akin to a man not wishing to believe that he will die, simply because the notion does not comfort him. Not only will he fail to prepare for death, as one ought to do, but he will inevitably find himself in the snare of death. Correct belief is not based on what we wish were true, but on Truth itself*[42]

LEO THE GREAT: ON CHRIST AS THE FULFILLMENT OF THE LAW, KNOWLEDGE OF WHICH CONTINUES TO BE OF VALUE FOR THOSE WHO LOVE HIM .

As, therefore, there is no one among the faithful to whom the gifts of grace are denied, so neither is there any among them not subject to the Christian rule of life. For though the harshness of the symbolic Law has been taken away, yet the gain from free obedience of the Law has increased, as John the Evangelist says, *For the Law was given by Moses; grace and truth came by Jesus Christ* (Jn 1:17). For everything that belonged to the Law, whether to circumcision, or to the different offerings, or to the observance of the Sabbath, all gave testimony to Christ, and foretold the grace of Christ.

And He is the *end of the Law* (Rom 10:4), not in that He brings it to nothing, but in that He fulfills it. And though He is the Author of both the New and the Old, He brought the mystical significance of the Figures and the Promises to an end, in that He fulfilled the promises and caused the prophecies to cease, since He who had been foretold had now come. But in the moral order there was no change in the precepts of the Old Law; rather many of them were enlarged through the Gospel teaching, that they might be clearer and more perfect teaching us salvation than they were when promising us a Savior.[43]

Chapter Two

ICON OF THE FOUR EVANGELISTS

This icon points to the second step in the salvation process: We must "Prove Belief." We prove we believe Christ is our Savior by trying to become like Him, with the guidance of the accounts of His Life written in the Gospels.

O Merciful Master, cause the pure light of the knowledge of You to shine in our hearts, and open the eyes of our minds to perceive Your message of good tidings; fill us with the fear of Your Blessed Commandments, that we, trampling down our fleshly desires, may seek a Heavenly citizenship and may do and consider all those things that are well pleasing to You.

For You, Christ our God, are the Source of Light to our souls and bodies, and to You we ascribe glory, with the Eternal Father, and the All Holy, Good and Life Giving Spirit, now and forever and from all ages to all ages. Amen.

(inaudible) Prayer before the Reading of the Gospel
Divine Liturgy of St. John Chrysostom

For the time will come when they will not endure sound doctrine, but according to their own desires, because they have itching ears, they will heap up for themselves teachers; and they will turn their ears away from the truth, and be turned aside to fables. But you be watchful in all things, endure afflictions, do the work of an evangelist, fulfill your ministry.

(2 Timothy 4:3-5)

Chapter Two
THE SECRET OF SALVATION

Perhaps each of you will say to himself: *I have believed, I shall be saved.* He speaks what is true if to faith he joins good works. That is indeed true faith which does not deny in work what it professes in word. For this Paul says of certain false faithful: *They profess that they know God; but in their works they deny Him* (Tit 1:16). For this John also says: *He who says that he knows God and keeps not His Commandments is a liar, and the truth is not in him* (1 Jn 2:4).

GREGORY THE GREAT

M.F. Toal, *The Sunday Sermons of the Great Fathers*

SALVATION IS A PROCESS

Orthodox theology preserves the truth that salvation is the process of sanctification: personal growth toward the image of God, following Christ's example (theosis). This process, made possible by grace, is fueled by faith and continues through and beyond our last breath on earth. We are saved by grace, through faith.

Jesus, the Sun of Justice, has arisen. The rays of this spiritual Sun spread out in all directions; and one indeed receives less grace, and another more; not that grace so gives itself, it is our own disposition that supplies the measure. For as the sun is one which gives light to the whole universe, and its ray is one, and its splendor, yet it does not shine with equal light upon all the world. Here is wondrous and abundant sunshine, here there is less. This house has little sunlight, this has it more abundantly; not because the sun gives more to this house and less to that, but according to the windows which were opened to it by those who build the houses it has more room to enter, and pours in accordingly. And since our thoughts and purposes are the windows of our soul, when you open wide your heart you receive a larger, more generous, divine favor; when you narrow your soul, you can but receive a less abundant grace. Open wide and lay bare your heart and soul to God, that His splendor may enter into you.

CHRYSOSTOM[1]

The process of salvation is synergistic. It is a cooperative effort between man and God, "which is simultaneously past, present and future."[2] As Orthodox Christians we say:

I WAS SAVED
(Heb 10:10)

when Jesus Christ died on the Cross to redeem me from my sins. He made my salvation possible. Before He did this, the only path to Heaven was through perfection through the Law[3]—an impossible feat.

That our Lord "paid" the penalty of death for our sins is not to be taken in the literal sense as a price exacted by and given in remuneration to someone but as the Savior accepting the painful consequences for the wrongful actions of others. When He took on flesh, the Son of God subjected Himself to death, which came to man as a result of sin. But Christ was sinless, so death could not hold Him. Likewise, under the terms of the Blood Covenant, death cannot hold anyone who is united with Christ through Baptism and Eucharist as part of a life of faith.

I AM SAVED
(Mt 13:35,
Eph 3:8-12)

in that I KNOW THE SECRET: that the way to the Kingdom is through Jesus Christ, the Son of God, Savior of all who turn to Him.[4] However, if, for example, I were studying the subject of math, I would not be allowed to just inform the teacher that I know the principles of that science and proceed to *take* a passing

28

grade! I would be given a test. In like manner, professed faith is not true faith unless it has been tested in the context of life. So, in the fullness of the truth, we go on to say ...

I AM BEING SAVED (present continuous) because I must demonstrate my faith in Christ as the Messiah in the way established by God: *by trying to become as much like Him as I can, through obedience.* Our Lord's perfect life set the example to follow.[5] This is a process. As St. Paul wrote, we must all press on toward the mark of perfection.[6] "We are always becoming what we already are potentially through faith and Baptism"[7]—a part of the Body of Christ. This ability is inherent in us as a hint from God, evident in the tendency of children to take on the characteristics of their heroes. This inner drive should be harnessed and directed toward a zealous effort to take on the qualities of our Savior, to show our love for and faith in Him and to prepare for life in His Kingdom, where all is holy.[8] The elements of the type of life this produces are the "good works" of the new covenant, which are very different from the legalistic works of the Mosaic Law. They can never *earn* us a place in Heaven but are, nevertheless, imperative as indicators of faith. They are also the means by which God wants His work to be done, with His people as His hands and feet, eyes and heart.[9] Works that are done other than as a result of faith have no spiritual value[10] because they produce only temporal benefits. Works done in the name of Jesus Christ and as fruit of

(Heb 10:14)

29

faith in Him produce benefits far beyond the obvious. The doer is blessed with grace, which strengthens him according to his efforts and helps him continue the works which prove his faith. The recipient of the benefits of the good works done in Christ's name receives, most importantly, a taste of the love that awaits him in the Kingdom, if he too believes. The "good" comes from pointing the Way to the Kingdom.

I WILL BE SAVED (Rom 10:9) when my life, my period of testing, is over or at the Second Coming of Christ, whichever occurs first. The instances of Enoch and Elijah being taken directly into Heaven are prefigurations of those who will still be alive at the Second Coming and who, belonging to Him, will not have to pass through death.[11] In either case, I must face Judgment[12] because only God (through His Son on the Throne of His Glory) can know whether I sincerely had faith in and love for Christ. My life will be evaluated not by successes or failures but by whether or not I truly tried, as a consequence of faith, to live a Christ-like life. To prove their love for God, Adam and Eve were expected to obey the one commandment God gave them. To prove our love for and belief in Jesus Christ as Savior, we are expected to attempt to follow His example in all things, as our acknowledgement of His existence and acceptance of Him as Lord and Master. Rev 20:12-13 clearly indicates that our faith is judged by our works.

30

Only one life—too soon will pass;
only what's done for God will last!

What role does God's grace play in our salvation?[13] Grace is the supernatural assistance given to man to sanctify him for the Kingdom. Positive action or attempt at action confirming faith is met concurrently by the Holy Spirit, Who grants grace according to our efforts.[14] Without grace, growth in Christ's image would not be possible.

> The grace of God is not able to visit those who flee salvation. Nor is human virtue of such power as to be adequate of itself to raise up to authentic life those souls who are untouched by grace...But when righteousness of works and the grace of the Spirit come together at the same time in the same soul, together they are able to fill it with blessed life.
> GREGORY OF NYSSA[15]

At the time of Judgment, grace will also compensate for the shortcomings of those whose lives, on balance, showed faith. God calls us to be perfect in imitation of our Lord to prove our faith and grow in His image (Holiness). He requires, however, only that we continually strive to do the best we can—His grace mercifully fills the gap.[16] So we continually pray: Kirie Eleison, Lord have mercy.

Christ's role in our salvation is objective. He did that which was necessary to make our union with God possible again. Our role is subjective. The *inner man* Paul wrote about[17] recognizes Christ as Messiah and exhibits faith on a mystical level through prayer, Baptism, Chrismation, Eucharist and the other Mysteries (Sacraments) of the Church. The *outer man* exhibits this faith on a moral level by showing love to others in a right relationship with God, following Christ's example.

Our salvation will become objective, "actualized," when we die. Our souls will immediately be judged and we will then receive, apart from our bodies, a foretaste of that for which we have prepared, much as we experience events in the dream state of sleep. If faith in Christ has manifested itself in the

31

pursuit of fellowship with Him through obedience, we will experience the joys of His presence. Then, at the Second Coming of Christ, we will be resurrected, with new bodies, and will enter the fullness of the Kingdom.

If pressed for an encapsulated answer to the question, "Are You Saved?" the most appropriate, concise response would be: "I AM BEING SAVED" (growing in sanctification by trying to live in obedience to Christ to prove my faith and love, which also prepares me for life in Heaven).[18] But we must strive to have a complete understanding of the all-encompassing stages of the process of salvation and be ready and eager to share this life-giving knowledge with others. To do so is the epitome of the type of love that Jesus practiced and taught.[19]

DANGER INHERENT IN "INSTANT SALVATION" THEORY

There are those who profess the so-called "instant salvation" theory, which is contrary to the witness of the early Church, thus to Orthodox theology. They cite Romans 10:9 as their biblical reference: *If you confess with your mouth the Lord Jesus and believe in your heart that God has raised Him from the dead, you will be saved.* That the only route to salvation is through faith in Jesus Christ as Savior is not a matter of contention. Orthodoxy parts company, however, with those who believe that this is an instantaneous event: that one need only orally proclaim Jesus as Lord, with the resultant right to say, "I AM SAVED!" Those who make this proclamation usually display a type of zeal which is both admirable and threatening. It is admirable in that child-like faith is exhibited, with the strength of conviction Peter displayed when he professed that Jesus is the Son of the Living God (which prompted our Lord to promise to build His Church on such rock-like faith).[20] It is threatening in that those who are exposed to it can either be drawn to the simplicity of it or offended by the aggression relative to it: *they have a zeal for God, but not according to knowledge* (Rom 10:2).

The simplicity implied may cause some to overlook the requirement to engage continually in the process of sanctification, as this theory bolsters the convictions of those who want to consider themselves Christians but don't want to have to try to live as Christ taught. They can then feel free to follow the ways of the world while fully expecting to go to Heaven when they die, confident that because Christ died for sinners there is no necessity for them to "do" anything other than that which pleases them. On the other hand, the aggressiveness of one who proclaims instant salvation, who often is very insistent that everyone must believe as he or she does, may cause others to become defensive and close their minds to the subject entirely. In either event, Satan will have accomplished his goal, which is to delay or prevent spiritual growth. The unqualified statement "I am saved!" is also reminiscent of the attitude of the Pharisee, whose voice resounded in praise of himself and whose arrogance and lack of humility Christ condemned. The repentant attitude of the tax collector who beat his breast and murmured, *God be merciful to me, a sinner,* drew the approval of Jesus, who said, *everyone who exalts himself will be abased, and he who humbles himself will be exalted* (Lk 18:9-14).

Scripture can only be correctly understood in its en tirety, not from fragments out of context. To insist on a literal interpretation of an isolated sentence here and there is to adhere to the *letter* but ignore its *spirit*,[21] which is what caused most of the Hebrew nation to reject Christ as their Messiah. To fully understand Romans 10:9, we must remember that St. Paul was addressing the Jews of Rome to try to help them understand that they were no longer dependent upon the Mosaic Law for salvation. The Law had been superseded by the Blood Covenant, whereby faith in Jesus Christ as Savior is the only criterion. However, Paul also plainly stated in Romans 3:31 that the Law was not abolished by Christ's coming but was fulfilled by it, as Matthew 5:17 makes clear in Jesus' own words.

We must grow in Christ's Image. The message of the Book of Romans, if taken in its entirety, is that if we truly believe that Christ is our Savior, we will learn that it is only by trying to live in imitation of Him that we demonstrate faith, and so **will be** saved (future tense). Imitating Christ includes loving one another as He loved us, the summation of the Ten Commandments and the Law.[22] It means giving of ourselves for others as He gave Himself for us. This requires physical

33

and spiritual struggle, so St. Paul also urges us to *endure hardship* like good soldiers and *compete according to the rules* like athletes (2 Timothy 2:3-5); to *put on the whole armor of God, that* [we] *may be able to stand against the wiles of the Devil* (Eph 6:11); and to *work out* [our] *own salvation with fear and trembling* (Phil 2:12). He makes the point that if we love Christ, *our salvation is **nearer** than when we first believed* (Rom 13:11), meaning that the longer we live "in Christ" (united with Him through Baptism, Eucharist and a life of faith), the closer we come to salvation, which is assured only when our life on earth is over and we have completed the test of faith. As long as we have life we can still stray from the road to God, but *He who endures to the end shall be saved* (Mk 13:13), receiving the *crown of life* from Christ Himself (Rev 2:10).

The instant salvation concept is formally known as "justification by faith alone."[23] Orthodox theology affirms that the believer is justified, declared guilt-free, by the intercessory saving acts of Christ but points ever beyond *justification* to *sanctification* by faith—through grace[24]—and rejects the word "alone," which carries with it the premise that no qualifying works or actions are required as demonstration or proof of faith. Martin Luther was a former Roman Catholic Priest who stressed justification by faith alone because of his grave concern about the legalistic overemphasis on works which had crept into the theology of the Roman Church (culminating in the sixteenth century with the selling of indulgences, which conveyed the impression that one could buy salvation). Luther's concerns were justified and his intentions good, but his theology (which marked the beginning of the Protestant Reformation) constituted a break in the crucial connection between professed faith and the essential elements of a Christ-like life (Jas 2:14-26).

"Justification by faith alone" usually encompasses either of two viewpoints: (1) After the proclamation of faith, good works will naturally follow, but are *not* necessary for salvation; or (2) After the proclamation of faith (considered a gift from God), the Holy Spirit will effect a change in one's life and *cause* him to grow in Christ's image.[25] The former is very ambiguous, lacking the sense of urgency that the early Church taught. Unfortunately, we usually do not automatically do what we should, unless we are convinced of its necessity. The latter puts the entire burden on God and none on us, and does not take free will into account. In contrast, the Old and New Testaments, from the examples of Adam and Eve to the blind man whose sight was not restored until he obeyed our Lord's command to *go and wash in the pool of Siloam* (Jn9:7,11), demonstrate the fact that God's plan for our salvation through faith in Jesus Christ as Messiah is in effect but requires that our faith be put into action and is subject to His judgment. The Book of Hebrews gives many examples of faith exhibited by people of God, citing instances when they *subdued kingdoms, worked righteousness, obtained promises, stopped the mouths of lions...* and *obtained a good testimony through faith...* (Heb 11:32-39). They did not just *say* they believed, they *proved* it by the way they lived (their works).

THE WAY TO PROVE BELIEF

The most important part of our work for God, and the way to demonstrate faith in and love for Christ, is to both *physically and spiritually* feed the hungry, give drink to the thirsty, welcome the stranger, clothe the naked, minister to the sick and visit the imprisoned.[26] Jesus Himself taught that whenever we help those in need, we are ministering to Him. This does not mean sporadic token activity. Doing God's work must become a way of life—*the Life in Christ*—and must touch all aspects of our daily activity. In our minds must always be the question, "In this situation, what would Jesus do?" Then we must *try* to act accordingly.

> *If a Christian,* Abba Agathon said, *kept the judgment which follows death in mind every moment, he would not sin with such ease.*[27]

Jesus said that if we are not *for* Him, we are *against* Him,[28] meaning that the Kingdom must be actively pursued. Indifference is the same as rejection. Rev 3:16 warns that God will spit the lukewarm out of His mouth because they do not even care enough to take a stand. God gives us life to make our choice and to demonstrate that choice in all our actions and decisions.

The fifth chapter of Romans describes the free gift that can be ours through faith in Jesus Christ, but the sixth chapter depicts the *newness of life* in which we must then walk, toward holiness and eternity with God (6:22). It tells us that we should *become slaves of God*. To say that we must prove our commitment to Christ is not to deny the fact that salvation is a gift from God. No amount of money can buy salvation, and we could never "do" enough to earn it. Clearly, then, if we can neither buy nor earn it, to those who receive it, salvation is a gift. Under the terms of God's Blood Covenant, this awesome gift is given to those whose lives show faith in Christ, undeserving though they are, for we would have to be absolutely without sin, as Jesus was, to deserve salvation.

The works which are the facets of a Christ-like life not only prove belief but also effect and indicate spiritual growth, which is impossible without works. The spiritual life is just that: life that is operating on the spiritual level—through prayer, meditation on God's truths, teaching His word, doing His work, giving of our time, talent and treasure, whoever and wherever we are. Those who take part in this life of faith continually grow in the image of God and develop an enriching, exciting relationship with Him that begins in this life and will continue to grow throughout eternity. That relationship will be reflected in a name He will write on a white stone that He will give to each of His beloved as they enter the fullness of His Kingdom.[29] In that blessed place there will be, however, no envy or competition because the special qualities of each relationship will be private—shared only with God.[30]

GREGORY THE GREAT **THE EVENT THAT OPENED THE GATES OF PARADISE**

.   ..however justly the Fathers lived before the Coming of the Lord, they were not brought into the Kingdom until Christ opened the gates of Paradise by the intervention of His death. They murmured because they had lived justly in order that they might enter the Kingdom, yet they suffered long delay before they entered it. They had labored in the Vineyard, yet the abodes of hell, however peaceful, had received them after their just lives...Not until after the long ages of hell did they reach, at last, the joys of the Kingdom. We, however, who have come at the eleventh hour murmur not after our labor...Because we came into this world after the Coming of the Mediator, we are brought into the Kingdom almost as soon as we depart from our body; and we receive without any delay that which the ancient Fathers merited to receive after prolonged delay.[31]

JOHN CHRYSOSTOM   **ON JUDGMENT**

Taking all these things into account and believing them in our heart: that after this present life we are to stand before a fearful tribunal, that we shall render an account of all we have done, that we shall receive sentence and suffer punishment if we remain in our sins, or that, on the other hand, we shall receive a crown and countless other good things if for this brief present time we have a care for our own souls, let us put to silence those who dare to say, to proclaim, what is contrary to this belief. Let us walk the paths of virtue, so that drawing near with a confident heart to that tribunal we may receive of the good things He has promised us, by the grace and mercy of our Lord Jesus Christ, to Whom be honor and glory now and forever. Amen.[32]

Chapter Three

ICON OF CHRIST, PANTOCRATOR

Christ, Pantocrator, ruler of All, Who will judge the living
and the dead by the truth found in the Gospels (Rom 2:16).
**This icon points to the third step in the salvation
process: We must *all* "Face Judgment."**

When he was about to die, the Holy Agathon remained in his bed motionless for three days, his eyes open and upturned towards Heaven. On the third day, when he recovered some, his disciples, who had assembled around him, asked him to tell them where his soul was during that interval of time.

Before the Judgment of God, he murmured, trembling.

And are you afraid, Father? the brothers asked with perplexity.

I tried, as best I could, to keep the laws of God all of my life. But I am a man. How do I know that I have pleased God? the holy one responded with great pain.

You are not sure that your works were pleasing to God? said the astonished monks.

Until I am before God, no, answered the holy one, *for man judges with one standard and God with another.*

The brothers wanted to ask other things for the benefit of their souls, but the holy one nodded to them not to speak any further.

I am preoccupied, his lips whispered.

His countenance began to shine! His disciples saw him leave this vain world for eternal life with the joy one feels when he sets off to meet his most beloved acquaintance.

Archimandrite Chrysostomos
The Ancient Fathers of the Desert

THE ROAD TO THE KINGDOM

The blessed Synkletike related to the Sisters that, *Those who begin the life in God encounter much toil and struggle in the beginning, afterwards, however, finding indescribable joy.*

For, she said, *just as those who wish to light a fire are at first choked by smoke and their eyes water from the fumes, yet later succeed at their task, so we who wish to light the divine fire within us must know that we will succeed at this only by many struggles and toil; for the Lord also says, "I came to cast fire upon the earth, and what else do I wish if the fire be more greatly kindled?"*

Indeed some , the blessed one continues, *while tolerating the bother and hindrance of the smoke in order to do a little work at the beginning, nonetheless, out of laziness, did not light a fire; for they went away quickly and did not have the forbearance to persist to the end.*

Archimandrite Chrysostomos
The Ancient Fathers of the Desert

IT IS *NOT* EASY

The road to God's Kingdom is often bumpy and sometimes hazardous,[1] but it leads to the *pearl of great price* (Mt 13:46). No effort is too great for such a glorious treasure. Our role in the process of salvation consists of four steps:

1. BELIEVE: acknowledge that Jesus Christ is the Son of God, our Savior, Who provides for us the only Way to the eternal presence of our Creator,[2] as we proclaim each time we recite the Nicene Creed:

I believe...in one Lord Jesus Christ, the only begotten Son of God, begotten of the Father before all ages...Who for us men and *for our salvation* came down from Heaven and was incarnated by the Holy Spirit and of the Virgin Mary and became man...

We may come to this acknowledgement at any time. As long as we have life, it is never too late to come to faith, if it is sincere.[3] But we never know when our life will end—death does not always announce itself in advance—so the sooner we address the issue of faith, the better.[4] Also, the more we delay, the more likely we are to stray so far from God that we may not even realize the need, or know how to "find Him" (Acts 17:27).

2. PROVE BELIEF: by trying to follow Jesus' example in all things throughout our lives. The Holy Mysteries (Sacraments) of the Church provide the basis for this life in Christ. They are outer symbols of inner grace received by those who submit to them—spiritual tools to help us reach our goal and to strengthen us for the struggle.

BAPTISM makes us a part of the Body of Christ, the Church.[5] The word *holy* means *set apart for God*. Baptism sets us apart as belonging to Him—*if* we try to live accordingly.[6] Just as physical birth from our mother's womb brought us into the world, our spiritual birth through Baptism puts us on the road to the Kingdom. At one point during this Sacrament the priest blows on the waters of the Baptismal Font—the breath of new life in Christ accessible through this Mystery.

> Jesus asks us to be born to a life different from that of all animals and other living things, a life which is the Life of God Himself. This life is given by the breath of God, which is the Holy Spirit of God (pnevma, in Greek, means both "breath" and "spirit"). God had already given this breath to us at Creation (Gen. 2:7), thus giving us His image, His freedom and the possibility to be more and more like Him through our own creative activity. Because of this breath, man is always called upon to surpass himself, so that he is truly man only when he participates in God's nature. Man loses this breath, this divine presence, through sin and death; but he can regain it in the water of Baptism, the source of Life.

Here in the baptismal water, sin, which is the cause of death, is drowned as if in the waters of the Flood or of the Red Sea. Here true Life springs forth, an eternal Life which God lives, communicated by the life-giving Holy Spirit. This is the Life which the Son of God came to give to us by yielding up His Spirit to the Father on the Cross and then rising from the dead to grant this same Spirit to those who believe in Him.[7]

Baptism is the beginning of our Christian walk, as it was the beginning of Jesus' public ministry. Through this Mystery, we are given the opportunity to free ourselves of the consequences of the sin of Adam and Eve and cleansed of any personal sins we may have committed. We are given a clean slate—our own opportunity for salvation. But as powerful and indispensable as Baptism is,[8] it is only the beginning—it gets us started.

If we come to Baptism willingly and lovingly after the age of reason, it is an indicator of our faith in Christ. St. Paul wrote that circumcision did not automatically confer righteousness upon the Jews under the Law. Rather, it was an outward sign, of merit only when the inner condition of the heart matched its meaning: commitment to keeping God's covenant with Moses while awaiting the Messiah.[9] So, similarly, Baptism for Christians is not a magical act guaranteeing a place in Heaven. It is, rather, the outward sign of inner grace received, the beginning of the process of sanctification for those who, thereafter, try to become more and more like Christ as they are able—a natural consequence of true faith but only with much discipline and effort.

Baptism, Chrismation, Eucharist and Unction are such important conveyors of grace that they are not denied to infants in the Orthodox Church. Through these Mysteries they receive vital spiritual nourishment for their souls while they are growing, just as we take steps to insure that they receive nourishment for their bodies before they understand the need for vitamins and minerals. If we were brought to Baptism as infants, it was an indicator of the faith of our parents and/or godparents, who then had the responsibility to nurture us spiritually as we grew. In a loving, faith-filled environment, who can say exactly when faith begins, and who can put limits on the power of grace? With maturity, the responsibility for spiritual growth becomes ours. We must be sure our Baptism has meaning for us. It is important to understand its significance and power; to remember the date of our Baptism and receive Holy Communion on each anniversary of that date; to wear a cross as a witness of our commitment to Christ (not as jewelry); to renew that commitment continually, especially during the Divine Liturgy, which gives us that opportunity many times by reminding us to "commit ourselves and one another, and our whole lives to Christ, our God"; and especially, to live that commitment.

CHRISMATION gives us the "seal of the gift of the Holy Spirit,"[10] the second element of the spiritual birth needed to enter the Kingdom, as Christ told Nicodemus.[11] A seal is a mark of authenticity. That which bears a particular seal conveys the authority it represents, as a document marked with the seal of a particular nation carries with it the power of that entity. Through the Sacrament of Chrismation we receive the Holy Spirit within us. The seal of this gift is set upon us and is operative to the extent we act accordingly (or others act on our behalf before we reach the age of reason). The more Christlike we become in cooperation with the Holy Spirit as He meets our efforts by strengthening, encouraging and directing us as we struggle along the steep and narrow road to the Kingdom, the more we act with the authority of God. This spiritual authority is recognizable to those who are in communion with Him.[12]

EUCHARIST (Holy Communion) allows us to partake of the very Body and Blood of Christ—a continual renewal of our union with Him and the strength it provides.[13] Through this Mystery we once again have access to the Tree of Life—the food of immortality—as part of the life in Christ.

> This Blood causes the image of our King to be fresh within us, produces beauty unspeakable, prevents the nobleness of our soul from wasting away, watering it continually and nourishing it...This Blood, **if rightly taken**, drives away devils and keeps them far from us, while it calls to us Angels and the Lord of Angels. For wherever they see the Lord's Blood,

44

devils flee, and Angels run together...This Blood is the salvation of our souls. By this the soul is washed, by this is beautiful, by this is inflamed. This causes our understanding to be more bright than fire and our soul more beaming than gold; this Blood was poured forth and made heaven accessible.

CHRYSOSTOM[14]

UNCTION is a tool for physical and spiritual healing. As the Book of James relates, we can ask our priests for the anointing and prayers of healing of this Sacrament at any time for a serious malady of body or soul,[15] to help us remain healthy and whole for our journey. Whenever we stray from the road leading to God (failing to follow Jesus' example in any way), the Church calls us to repentance. Through the Mystery of *CONFESSION* we can receive forgiveness and renewal. All confessed sins for which we are truly repentant (including indifference toward God) are erased.[16] A sincere confession restores the sin-free state of the newly Baptized—we are born anew from above spiritually and put back on the road to God. In the case of serious sin, a drastic falling away, Confession can have dramatic and life-changing results. It gives us a way to eliminate the barriers (that sins form) between us and God—a chance to get back to the real purpose for life.

If we choose to have a partner accompany us on the road to God (hopefully to include being a spiritual helpmate), the Church offers the Mystery of *MARRIAGE*, to bless and sanctify our union.[17] God's plan calls for new, human life to be brought forth within the state of marriage between a man and a woman to provide for the nurturing of souls for His Kingdom.[18] In a good marriage, one party can provide what the other lacks. Together man and woman are whole in a way not possible for either alone, reflecting the wholeness of God.

Those males who receive a special calling from God are offered *ORDINATION* for a life of service, to bring as many as possible to Christ and help them remain in the fold. This is not the Levitical priesthood of the Old Testament, established to offer atoning sacrifices of the people to God under the Mosaic Law, but the high priesthood of Christ Himself, after the order of Melchizedek,[19] which is eternal, and continually offers to

45

God, sacramentally, the one, final blood sacrifice of Christ in redemption of the sins of mankind. The priest "can fulfill this service only because the priesthood...is not 'his'...but the one and same indivisible priesthood of Christ, which eternally lives and is eternally fulfilled in the Church, the Body of Christ."[20]

In addition, the Church offers the spiritual tools of *prayer, fasting, worship, fellowship and knowledge* (Holy Tradition—which includes Holy Scripture, writings of the Fathers of the Church and Councils, Iconography, Liturgics, etc.—all the vehicles that have been employed to preserve the truth about Christ) to help us in our endeavor to grow in holiness as part of God's Kingdom.

3. FACE JUDGMENT. Each of us will be judged by that which we were able to learn and understand about what God expects of us and the extent to which we tried to live accordingly.[21] To some has been given the privilege and responsibility of insight into the hidden mysteries of God.[22] He will expect much from them in terms Christ-like lives and resultant souls brought to Him. To others, perhaps only a glimmer of God's Light has been able to penetrate the barriers erected by Satan. Each will be judged fairly by Christ, Who is All-Knowing, All-Loving, All-Just. Awareness of the fact that we must face judgment is a blessing because it helps us prevent spiritual negligence.

In a sense we will judge ourselves: the way in which we judge others will be the standard by which we will be judged,[23] and when the *Book of Life* is opened (Rev 20:12-13) we will have total recall of our lives. We will not have to be told where we stand in our relationship with God—we will *know*.

> The wicked will understand how great a salvation they rejected, how great a love and mercy they scorned in life, and for them, [the] radiant love and glory of God, from which they can no longer hide, becomes as a river of fire, pouring forth from the glory or throne of Christ, and it sweeps them away, their conscience receiving it as coals of fire. The righteous receive one and the same "fire" as complete spiritual illumination and understanding and are filled with unspeakable joy and exaltation by it,

for this fire shall be to them the rays of the Sun of righteousness which shall heal them of all that they lack, and they shall go forth and grow in perfection and knowledge unto all eternity...(Mal 4:1-2)[24]

Of those who profess instant salvation, or salvation by faith alone, some ignore the idea of judgment and emphasize the Resurrection when, it is said, the *SAVED* will be resurrected to God's Kingdom and the *UNSAVED* to damnation.[25] In other words, it is considered that there will be no actual time of judgment, for those who have announced themselves "saved" *are*, while the rest are damned. But this theory is based on erroneous worldly rationalization, not on the enlightenment that God will provide at Christ's Second Coming. Others say judgment is for the saved only, whose Christian lives will be assessed to disclose what has been "valuable to God's Kingdom" and what has been "worthless,"[26] affecting their placement in Heaven. But Paul writes that *we must **all** appear before the judgment seat of Christ* and refers to the *terror of the Lord* (2 Cor 5:10-11). Is there to be punishment in Heaven? If we are saved instantaneously, by profession of faith only, why need we worry about judgment for placement? Any place in Heaven would be wondrous.[27]

There will indeed be judgment, but the sincere Christian need not despair. We should not live our lives in doubt and trepidation because we have the *hope* of salvation.[28] We know that God keeps His promises, and that if we truly love Him and really try to be followers of Christ, we *shall be saved* (Mt 24:13). The Day of Judgment will be no problem for true lovers of Christ. They will sail through the process, finding no condemnation but passing *from death to life* (Jn 5:24). This knowledge can serve to fill us with deep, inner joy, no matter what ups and downs our earthly life brings.[29]

The Christian on the road to salvation, the road which leads to personal unity with God, must constantly find himself between fear and hope. Fear restrains us, yet at the same time it pushes us toward God. Hope fills us with power and draws us toward the love of the Father.[30]

47

4. RECEIVE REWARD. Those whose lives have demonstrated faith that Jesus is the Son of the Living God, Savior of the world, will be invited to enter fully into the Kingdom of eternal joy prepared for them from the foundation of the world.[31] God will call each of them by name and give them the Crown of Life[32] and the white stone with His special name for them written on it. In that blessed place there will be no more death, no more sorrow, no more crying, no more pain.[33] The Kingdom begins in this life for those Baptized Christians who commit their lives to Christ because they live with the joy of knowing the certainty of God's promises. As soon as real faith begins, the believer actually begins to experience God's Kingdom—while still on earth. To the extent worldly life is rejected, spiritual life flourishes and its *fruit* is tasted (Gal 5:22).

> As wickedness tends to punish those who pursue it even before they arrive at the pit, so also virtue, even before the gift of the Kingdom, provides delights for those who practice it on earth, so they live in company with good hopes and continual pleasure.   CHRYSOSTOM[34]

God created us to live forever—and so we will—in one situation or another. Those whose lives have not demonstrated faith in Christ as Savior (if they were exposed to this saving truth) will endure eternal agony with Satan and his followers,[35] far removed from *the presence of God and the glory of His power* (2 Thess 1:9).

> We cannot imagine what it will be like to be deprived of that Blessed Glory, to be hated by Christ, to hear *I do not know you* (Mt 25:12).   CHRYSOSTOM[36]

This is not punishment inflicted by God but rather the natural consequence of rejecting Him.[37] We are granted that which we have chosen.

NARROW IS THE GATE and difficult is the Way which leads to Life, and there are few who find it (Mt 7:14). The endeavor to live a Christ-like life can be likened to an uphill climb on a steep mountain road. Inching our way upward through the joys and pitfalls of life, the narrow gate into the fullness of the glorious Kingdom of God is our destination. We are put on this road at Baptism, with our eyes fixed on our Savior. The Holy Spirit lovingly nudges us along throughout our lives at a pace determined by our love and faith. The tools provided by the Church help us along the way, with sincere repentance and the Sacrament of Confession renewing us and putting us back on the road when we stray.

We're all different. We each start out in a different environment for our climb. Some enjoy an atmosphere of love, mature guidance and material comforts. Others struggle with deprivation of all sorts. Some are blessed with fertile spiritual soil in which to grow and begin the process early; other souls gasp for breath in a spiritual wasteland and are not awakened to God until late in life. All sorts of scenarios are possible. As we have not been given the same resources for our journey through life, God does not expect the same from each of us. Along with free will, we have each been given the opportunity to respond to God in our own unique way. He demands, for our own good, only that we use that which we have been given in His service,[38] in accordance with His word. He will judge accordingly. It does not matter how far along on the road to perfection our struggle takes us, only whether we have the love for God and faith in His Son as Savior to really *try* to continue the ascent until the end of our lives.

God does not promise that we will not encounter difficulties in life. He does promise to be with us, to guide and strengthen us, and to help us complete the journey.[39] He allows us to feel His love through glimpses into the Kingdom that are so glorious and powerful that we thirst for more. These glimpses are sometimes given through an enhanced awareness of the beauty of God's creation, hinting at the glories waiting in Heaven.[40] They may also come during times of suffering, when we become aware of our complete dependence on God's mercy in those things that really matter, and when, having exhausted our human means of coping, we can actually feel His presence sustaining us, comforting us.[41]

EPHRAEM THE SYRIAN   ON THE JOY
OF ENTERING THE KINGDOM
AND THE AGONY OF BEING EXCLUDED

With what joy shall we be filled, if we are directed to the right hand of the King? What must we be like when the Just embrace us there? ...Abraham, Isaac, Jacob, Moses, Noah, Job, Daniel, the holy Prophets, the Apostles, the Martyrs, who were all pleasing to God in the days of the flesh? And whomsoever you have heard of, and whose life you have admired, and whom you now wish to see, they will come to you, and embrace you, rejoicing in your salvation. What kind of men must we be? Of what kind shall be that unspeakable delight which we are to receive, when the King shall with joyfulness say to those who will be on His right hand: *Come you blessed of my Father, possess the Kingdom prepared for you from the foundation of the world* (Mt 25:34).

Then you will receive the Kingdom of beauty, the Crown of all your desires, from the Hand of the Lord, and reign with Christ forever. Then you will receive for your inheritance the gifts *which God has promised to those who love and serve Him* (Jas 1:12). From then forward you will be secure, no longer filled with anxiety. Be mindful of what kind of a person it must be, to whom it will be given to reign with Christ in Heaven. Reflect upon what it means to dwell forever in the light of His Countenance, to possess the source of all light. *For then you shall no longer have the sun for your light by day, neither shall the brightness of the moon enlighten you* (Isa 60:19), but Christ will be your unfailing Light and God your glory. Behold what glory He has laid up for those who fear Him, observing His Commandments.

Then think about the end of sinners as they are led before that tremendous tribunal. What terror will lay hold of them in the presence of that just Judge, having now no way to escape His presence? What shame will seize them as they are turned towards the left hand of the King? What dread gloom will fall upon them, when in His anger He shall speak to them, and trouble them in His rage, saying: *Depart from me, you cursed, into everlasting fire, which was prepared for the Devil and his angels* (Mt 25:41).[42]

GREGORY THE GREAT   ON NOT JUDGING
OURSELVES OR OTHERS

Many come to faith, but few are brought into the Heavenly Kingdom. And many serve God with their tongue but turn from Him in their lives. From this we should reflect on two things. The first is that no one should presume concerning his own salvation because though he is called to the faith he does not know whether he will be chosen to enter the Kingdom of Heaven. The second is that no one should take it upon himself to despair of the neighbor he sees steeped in vice because no one knows the richness of divine mercy.[43]

ICON OF
CHRIST'S DESCENT INTO HADES

This icon points to the fourth step in the salvation process: "Receive Reward." We will receive that which we have chosen. Those whose lives showed faith in Christ as the One who gave them the Way back to union with God will be part of His Kingdom—eternally.

While the Body of Jesus Christ lay in the Tomb, His Soul descended into Hades (1Pet 4:6 and Eph 4:9-10) to give those who had lived and died before His redeeming death released man from the bondage of Satan the opportunity to recognize and accept Him as the Messiah of Old Testament prophesy. Thus the icon of *Christ's Descent into Hades* (also known as the *Resurrection*) depicts Him trampling upon the gates of Hades, and Adam and Eve (representing mankind) being freed from the throes of death. The figure shown in chains in the blackness at the bottom is the Devil, illustrating the fact that his power had now been harnessed. The hold he had over mankind was death—but it has lost its "sting": though man still has to pass through death (until the Second Coming), it cannot hold those who belong to Christ. Surrounding Christ are figures from the Bible who lived and died before His Death opened the Gates of Paradise: on His right, Kings David and Solomon and John the Baptist; on His left, Abel (who foreshadowed Christ) and the prophets.[44]

> Going down to death, O Life immortal, You have slain Hell with the dazzling light of Your divinity. And when You had raised up the dead from their dwelling place beneath the earth, all the powers of Heaven cried aloud: *Giver of Life, O Christ our God, glory to You.*
> Troparion from Great Saturday's Matins
> Kallistos Ware and Mother Mary
> *The Lenten Triodion*

The cover of this book features another rendition of the icon of *Christ's Descent into Hades*. It depicts His Soul leaving His reposing Body in the Tomb and descending into Hades. The outstretched hands are of those in Hades who had been desperately awaiting the Messiah. They graphically reflect the believer's recognition of Christ as his or her only salvation.

> Being God, you were present in the grave bodily; but in Hades with the Soul; in Paradise with the thief; and on the throne with the Father and the Spirit, fulfilling all things, yet enscribed by none.
> From the Service of Proskomide
> *The Order of The Divine and Holy Liturgy*
> Holy Cross Orthodox Press

EPILOGUE

ARE YOU SAVED? is a question that should be of primary concern to all who have received the gift of life. This work is an effort to provide, in layman's terms, a sketch of God's divine plan for His beloved "man," so that those who seek knowledge of the purpose for life may be guided by His Truth, which remains the same in every time and in every place.

The message of salvation through the Son of God is for everyone. It is simple and all encompassing. It should be shouted from the rooftops and taught again and again in our homes and churches at every level of human understanding. It should permeate every area of our lives and guide every action and decision.

The precepts put forth in this work have been taught by the historic Church since Jesus Christ ascended into Heaven to wait for those who love Him. The accompanying prayer is that this telling will help some to understand what Christ has done for us and thus inspire them to make and/or continually renew a serious, life-giving commitment to Him as Lord and Savior. May we all work together to share this life-giving knowledge with all who will listen, and may we all continue to *grow in His image* to show our faith in and love for Him, in readiness for the holiness of His Kingdom.

NOTES

Chapter One

1. Gen 1:28.
2. Gen 3:8-9.
3. Fr. Kallistos Ware, *The Orthodox Way*, p.66.
4. Isa 14:12-21, Rev 12:7-12.
5. Philip Schaff, "The Second oration on Easter," *Nicene and Post Nicene Fathers of the Christian Church,* Vol. VII, p.425.
6. Panayiotis Nellas, "Garments of Skin," *Deification in Christ*, p.46-53.
7. Gen 3:17-19.
8. "The Orthodox Church has always repudiated the doctrine of 'original guilt'—that is, the view that all men share not only the consequences of but also the guilt for the sin of Adam and Eve." Cronk, p.45. Also see Ware, p.80-81.
9. Rev 21:3-4.
10. Nikolaos P. Vassiliadis, *The Mystery of Death*, p.519-520.
11. Gen 3.15.
12. Jn 8:44.
13. Rev. George Nicozisin & Presbytera Freida Upson, *The Sacraments of the Orthodox Church*, p.7-10.
14. Gen 17:1-2.
15. Vladimir Lossky, *Orthodox Theology, An Introduction*, p.86.
16. Rom 3:19-20.
17. Ex 34:27-28.
18. See Books of Exodus, Leviticus, Numbers and Deuteronomy.
19. Deut 27:10, 26; Jas 2:10.
20. 1 Jn 2:2.
21. Ex 25:22.
22. Lev 16.
23. Ex 26:33.
24. Heb 9:1-15.
25. Gen 5:24; Heb 11:5; II Kings 2:1-11.
26. M. F. Toal, *The Sunday Sermons of the Great Fathers,* vol. two, p.54-55.
27. Mt 5:48.
28. "In order for Christ to save His people He must be a theanthropos—a divine and human being. He must be God to be able to save, and He must be man so that salvation can be real on behalf of mankind and not merely of God, from above only, as a sort

of magical salvation." Bishop Gerasimos Papadopoulos, *Orthodoxy: Faith and Life,* vol. two, *Christ in the Life of the Church,* p.41.

29. Gen 28:12-13; Jn 1:51.

30. Jn 7:30, 8:20; 10:31,39.

31. Jn 17:1.

32. Jn 10:17-18.

33. Lossky, "Christological Dogma," *Theology,* p.114.

34. R. Payne Smith, trans., "On the Incarnation," *Commentary on the Gospel of St. Luke, note 1, p.52.*

35. Gen 22:7-8; Ex 12:3-13; Lev 23:12; Isa 53:7; Jn 1:29.

36. Mt 27:51-54; Lk 23:44-45.

37. Toal, "On the Holy Pasch," vol. two, p.257.

38. 1 Cor 15:20.

39. Heb 9:14-15 (read Chapters 8 through 10).

40. Eph 2:4-6; Gal 4:4-7.

41. Nikolai Velimirovic, *The Prologue from Ochrid*, Part One, p.296.

42. Archimandrite Chrysostomos, *The Ancient Fathers of the Desert*, p.66.

43. Toal, vol. two, p.151.

Chapter Two

1. Toal, "On the Gospel," vol. one, p.417.

2. George Cronk, *The Message of the Bible, An Orthodox Christian Perspective*, p.265.

3. Rom 4:13-15, 7:7-8:4.

4. Jn 14:6.

5. 1 Pet 2:21.

6. Phil 3:12-16.

7. Papadopoulos, p. 56.

8. Heb 12:14

9. 1 Cor 12:27.

10. Heb 11:6.

11. 1 Thess 4:15-18.

12. Jn 5:26-30.

13. Eph 2:8-10.

14. Archimandrite Christoforos Stavropoulos, *Partakers of Divine Nature*, trans. The Rev. Dr. Stanley S. Harakas, p.35.

15. ibid, p.34.

16. Tit 3:4-7.

17. 1 Cor 2:11.

18. Heb 5:8-9.

19. Jn 15:9-17.

20. Mt 16:13-18.

21. 2 Cor 3:6

22. Rom 13:8-10.

23. It is commonly thought that this theory originated at the time of the Protestant Reformation, with Martin Luther, but it was actually one of the heresies of the first century. Most of the Book of James was written as a refutation of this heresy. See Cronk, p.233.

24. Rom 3:23-26; 2 Thess 2:13-17.

25. J. Leslie Dunstan, *Protestantism*, p.208-10.

26. Mt 25:31-46.

27. Chrysostomos, p.94.

28. Mt 12:30.

29. Rev 2:17.

30. Ware, p.183-185.

31. Toal, vol. one, p.382.

32. ibid, vol. two, p.25.

Chapter Three

1. Mt 11:12.

2. Jn 14:6; 1 Tim 2:4-5.

3. Mt 20:1-16.

4. Mk 9:36-37, 10:13-16.

5. 1 Cor 12:13.

6. Col 1:18-23.

7. Olga Dunlop, *The Living God*, vol. 1, p.223.

8. Mt 3:13-15, 28:18-20; Jn 3:5.

9. Rom 2:25-29, 4:11-12.

10. The "seal" is conveyed by the consecrated myrrh used in the Sacrament of Chrismation. 2 Cor 1:21-22; 1 Jn 2:20.

11. Jn 3:5.

12. 1 Cor 2:4-5.

13. Mt 26:26-28; Lk 22:19-20; Jn 6:56.

14. Philip Schaff, "Homily XLVI of the Gospel of John," *Nicene and Post Nicene Fathers of the Christian Church*, Vol. XIV, p.166-167.

15. Jas 5:13-15.

16. Jn 20:23.

17. Gen 2:24; Mt 19:4-6.

18.Gen 1:27-28.

19. Gen 14:18; Ps 110:4; Heb 4:14-7:28; Mk 3:14-15; Mt 28:16-20.

20. Alexander Schmemann, *The Eucharist*, p.115.

21. Rom 2:1-16.

22. 1 Cor 2:6-7.

23. Mt 7:1-2.

24. Lazar Puhalo, *The Soul, the Body and Death*, p.45.

25. Jerry Falwell, ed., with Ed Dobson and Ed Hindson, *The Fundamentalist Phenomenon, The Resurgence of Conservative Christianity*, p.21.

26. D. Guthrie, *The New Bible Commentary*, p.1080.

27. Ps 84:10.

28. Rom 8:24.

29. "Orthodoxy believes that salvation is not so much a negative reality as it is a positive one: salvation is not so much to be freed from the bondage of the devil and his dominion of sin, death and corruption as it is life in communion with God." Maximos Aghiorgoussis, "The Theology and Experience of Salvation," *The Greek Orthodox Theological Review*, Vol. XXII, Winter 1977, No. 4, p.414.

30. Archimandrite Christoforos Stavropoulos, *Partakers of Divine Nature*, p.54.

31. Mt 25:34.

32. Jas 1:12; Rev 3:5.

33. Rev 21:4.

34. Schaff, "Homily XL," p.147.

35. Mt 25:41.

36. Schaff, "Homily XXIII on Matthew," *NPNF* Vol.X, p.164.

37. Jn 12:48.

38. Rom 12:4-8.

39. Mt 28:20; 2 Cor 1:3-5.

40. Rom 1:19-20.

41. 2 Cor 1:8-10.

42. Toal, vol. one, p.13.

43. ibid, p.365.

44. Photios Kontoglou, *Ekphrasis*, p. 180.

Scriptural references throughout this work were taken from *The New King James Version* of the *Holy Bible* (Thomas Nelson, Inc., 1982).

BIBLIOGRAPHY

Aghiorgoussis, Maximos, "The Theology and Experience of Salvation," *The Greek Orthodox Theological Review*, Vol. XXII, Winter 1977, No.4.

Anderson, David and John Erickson. *The Services of Christmas, The Nativity of our Lord God and Savior Jesus Christ*. Syosset, New York: Orthodox Church in America, 1981.

Backman, Milton V. Jr. *Christian Churches of America, Origins and Beliefs*. Utah: Brigham Young University Press, 1976.

Bettenson, Henry, ed. *The Early Christian Fathers*. London: Oxford University Press, 1956.

Chrysostomos, Archimandrite, trans. "The Evergetinos on Passions and Perfection in Christ," *The Ancient Fathers of the Desert*. Brookline: Hellenic College Press, 1980

Cronk, George. *The Message of the Bible, An Orthodox Perspective*. Crestwood, New York: St. Vladimir's Seminary Press, 1982.

Dunlop, Olga. *The Living God, A Catechism for the Christian Faith*. Two volumes. Crestwood, New York: St. Vladimir's Seminary Press, 1989.

Dunstan, J. Leslie, ed. *Protestantism*. New York: George Braziller, 1962.

Falwell, Jerry, ed. with Ed Dobson and Ed Hindson. *The Fundamentalist Phenomenon*. New York: Doubleday & Company, Inc., 1981.

Guthrie, D., J.A. Motyer, A.M. Stibbs, D.J. Wiseman, eds. *The New Bible Commentary, Rev.* Grand Rapids, Michigan: Wm. B. Eerdman's Publishing Company, 1970.

Halley, Henry H. *Halley's Bible Handbook*, 24th ed. Grand Rapids, Michigan: Zondervan Publishing House, 1965.

Haverstick, John. *The Progress of the Protestant, A Pictorial History from the Early Reformers to Present Day Ecumenism.* New York/Chicago/San Francisco: Holt, Rinehart and Winston, 1968.

Kontoglou, Photios. *Ekphrasis*, 3rd ed.,Vol.1. Athens: Astir Press, 1993.

Lossky, Vladimir. *Orthodox Theology, An Introduction.* Crestwood, New York: St. Vladimir's Seminary Press, 1978.

Mary, Mother and Archimandrite Kallistos Ware. *The Lenten Triodion.* South Canaan, Pennsylvania: St. Tikhon's Seminary Press, 1994.

Nellas, Panayiotis. *Deification in Christ, The Nature of the Human Person.* Crestwood, New York: St.Vladimir's Seminary Press, 1987.

Nicozisin, George and Freida Upson. *The Sacraments of the Orthodox Church.* Greek Orthodox Archdiocese of North and South America, 1973.

The Order of the Divine and Holy Liturgy. Brookline, Massachusetts: Holy Cross Orthodox Press, 1987.

Papadopoulos, Gerasimos. *Orthodoxy: Faith and Life, Christ in the Life of the Church.* Brookline, Mass: Holy Cross Orthodox Press, 1981.

Puhalo, Lazar. *The Soul, the Body and Death.* Canada: Synaxis Press, 1985.

Schaff, Philip, & Henry Wace, ed. Gregory Nazianzen: "The Second Oration on Easter," *Nicene and Post Nicene Fathers of the Christian Church*, Vol. VII, Grand Rapids, Michigan: Wm. B. Eerdman's Publ. Company, 1989.

Schaff, Chrysostom: "Homilies on the Gospel of St. Matthew," Vol. X, 1991.

_____, Chrysostom: "Homilies on the Gospel of St. John & the Epistle to the Hebrews," Vol. XIV, 1989.

Schmemann, Alexander. *The Eucharist.* Crestwood, New York: St. Vladimir's Seminary Press, 1988.

Smith, R. Payne, trans. *Commentary on the Gospel of St. Luke, by St. Cyril of Alexandria,* Studion Publishers, 1983.

Stavropoulos, Christoforos. *Partakers of Divine Nature.* trans. Stanley Harakas. Minneapolis: Light and Life Publishing Company, 1976.

Toal, M.F., trans and ed. *The Sunday Sermons of the Great Fathers.* Four volumes. Chicago: Henry Regnery Co. London: Longmans, Green, 1957.

Vassiliadis, Nikolaos P. *The Mystery of Death.* trans. Fr. Peter A. Chamberas. Athens: The Orthodox Brotherhood of Theologians, "The Savior," 1993.

Velimirovic, Bishop Nikolai. *The Prologue From Ochrid, Lives of the Saints and Homilies for Every Day in the Year.* trans. Mother Maria. Four parts. Birmingham, England: Lazarica Press, 1985.

Ware, Kallistos. *The Orthodox Way.* Crestwood, New York: St. Vladimir's Orthodox Theological Seminary, 1979.

Ware, Timothy. *The Orthodox Church.* Middlesex, England; Baltimore: Penguin Books, Inc., 1963.